JOHN THE BAPTIST

- Was Jesus' cousin
- Baptized many people, including Jesus
- Wore clothes made of camel's hair and ate locusts and honey

BOY WITH LOAVES AND FISH

- Was part of the crowd listening to Jesus teach
- Spoke to the grown-ups to see if he could help solve the dinner problem
- Was willing to share all he had so other people wouldn't be hungry

GOOD SAMARITAN

- Took care of a hurting man who was considered his enemy
- Put the man on his donkey and carried him to an inn
- Paid for everything the man needed to get well

TABITHA

- Paid attention to people who needed things
- Spent time making clothes she could give away
- Became known for helping the poor

PRISCILLA

- Was close friends with Paul
- Shared her home so people could meet to worship God
- Helped many people grow closer to Jesus

JESUS

- Fulfilled Old Testament prophecies (matched up exactly with what God had said the Savior would be)
- Is the Son of God from heaven, sent to the world to show what God is like and to rescue people from their sin
- Died on the cross and rose from the dead to make a way for people to be forgiven and have life with God forever

Little Faithfuls
You're So Kind

Written by Carrie Marrs
Illustrated by Christiane Engel

God's big story of kindness started long ago, before any of us were born. When there was no land or sky or animals, God created the whole world out of kindness.

He made people so that He could love them and they could love Him back.

He made bright sunshine to play in, sweet apples to munch on, and fuzzy kittens to cuddle. He made these things to take care of us and make us smile.

God also designed the world so its parts would help each other—like how flowers give bees nectar to eat and how those bees spread pollen to flowers to help them grow.

People are meant to help each other too.

Not long after God made the world, some special people found ways to spread His kindness to the people around them.

Joseph was one of those special people. He had ten mean older brothers who sent him away to work as a slave in Egypt. Joseph's life was hard for many years, but then he ended up becoming someone in charge. Only the king of Egypt, known as Pharaoh, was more important than him!

One day back home, Joseph's family ran out of food. So they went to Egypt to ask for help—which meant asking Joseph for help.

Even though his brothers had treated him unfairly all those years ago, Joseph chose to be kind. "I forgive you," he said. "I'll take care of you and give you food."

Years after Joseph lived, there was a new pharaoh in Egypt who didn't like the Israelites, who are God's chosen people. Pharaoh wanted to get rid of all the Israelites' baby boys. One mother saved her baby, Moses, by hiding him in a basket and putting the basket on a river. Moses' sister, Miriam, followed the basket to see what would happen.

Pharaoh's daughter found Moses in the basket and decided to adopt him. Miriam walked up to her and asked, "Should I go get someone to help take care of him?" She knew her mother would love to do that! Pharaoh's daughter said yes.

Miriam had made sure her baby brother was protected and loved.

When Moses grew up, God gave him a big job. Moses was supposed to tell Pharaoh to let the Israelites leave Egypt. Moses wasn't very good at speaking though. So his brother, Aaron, said, "I'll come with you. I'll say whatever you have trouble saying."

Aaron became Moses' loyal helper, standing shoulder to shoulder with him as he stood up to Pharaoh. Together they trusted and obeyed God, and God freed the Israelites.

Years later, there lived a woman named Naomi. After Naomi's husband and two grown-up sons died, she was so sad. Naomi said to her sons' wives, "I have to go to my hometown, Bethlehem, because I have no money for food here."

The two women had to choose if they would stay with Naomi. One of the women, Orpah, said good-bye and left. But the other woman, Ruth, said, "I don't want you to feel alone, so I'm going to stay with you—forever."

In Bethlehem, Ruth worked in the fields so that she and Naomi would have food to eat. She also got married and had a baby! Because of Ruth's kindness, she and Naomi became happy again.

Ruth's great-grandson was named David, and one day he found himself in danger. David had been chosen by God as the next king of Israel. That made Saul, who was already king, angry. He tried to hurt David.

Jonathan, the king's son, would normally have been the next king. He could have been jealous of David. But instead, Jonathan loved David. They were best friends.

"I'll help you stay safe from my father," Jonathan told David. "And I'll give you some of my most special things—my royal robe, armor, and sword."

Because Jonathan cared more about his friend than about becoming the next king, he made their friendship even stronger. He even saved David's life, and David became one of the greatest kings of God's people.

Later on, David and an army of men were protecting a flock of sheep that belonged to Nabal. When it was time for Nabal to give them food as a thank-you for their help, he wouldn't do it. David got so mad that he told his army, "Get out your swords!"

Nabal's wife, Abigail, heard about what happened. She thought, *Nabal wasn't kind, but I can be!*

She brought enough food for six hundred men to David and said, "I'm sorry about what my husband did. I hope we can find a way to be friends."

Abigail's kindness softened David's heart. "Thank you," he said. "There will be no battle today."

David had a son who grew up and had a baby. Then that baby grew up and had a baby. On and on it went, for many years, until Jesus was born. When Jesus grew up, John the Baptist helped people get ready to meet Him.

John told people, "God loves you so much that He's sending His Son to rescue you." Big crowds surrounded John and wanted to follow him.

But John said, "Don't follow me—I'm not the rescuer. I'm the messenger. Someone much more powerful is coming after me."

And when Jesus showed up, John didn't try to keep the crowd focused on himself. He was ready to become less important. He said, "This is God's chosen one. Follow Him!"

Those crowds did begin following Jesus. One day everyone listened to Him teach for so long that their bellies started growling—and they were far from a village where they could buy dinner.

A little boy offered to help. "I have five loaves of bread and two fish," he said. "I know it's not a lot, but I'm happy to share it."

Jesus took what the boy offered and did something amazing with it. He turned it into enough food for the entire crowd—more than five thousand people!

The boy's small act of kindness made a *big* difference.

One time when Jesus was teaching, He talked about being kind to everyone, even to people who are mean. He told a story with a sad beginning: a Jewish man was robbed, beaten, and left on the side of the road.

When a couple of Jewish people saw the man, they ignored him.

But when a Samaritan man found him, he took care of him. The Jews and Samaritans didn't usually get along. The Samaritan man could have thought, *He wouldn't help me, so I'm not going to help him.*

Instead, he said, "I'll bandage your wounds, take you to a comfy place to rest, and pay for whatever else you need."

Jesus' story of the good Samaritan showed people how to be kind to everyone they meet.

After Jesus went to heaven, people who believed in Him started living like Him. One of those people was named Tabitha.

Tabitha paid special attention to people who didn't have what they needed—some were hungry and thirsty. Others didn't have enough clothes or a home. She thought, *If I were one of them, what would I want someone to do for me?*

Then she found a way to help. She was good at sewing, so she made clothes and gave them away. Because of her kindness, many people had enough clothes to wear!

Priscilla was another person who believed in Jesus and lived like Him.

She and her husband were tentmakers, and one day they met another tentmaker—the apostle Paul. They all became good friends.

Priscilla found out that Paul had nowhere to live. She said, "We have a house nearby. You can come over and stay as long as you want!"

"Really?" said Paul. "I would love that. Thank you!"

So Paul had a place to rest, eat meals, and have happy times with friends—all because Priscilla was willing to share her home. He was so glad to be there that he ended up staying for more than a year.

Ever since those first believers, Jesus' followers have remembered how kind Jesus was when He was with them. He always showed people they were important to God.

To Zacchaeus, whom everyone disliked, He said, "I'll come to your house and share a meal with you."

To a man with a skin disease, whom everyone was afraid to touch, He said, "I'll touch you and help you."

To the children who were feeling left out, He said, "Come here. I'll give you a big hug and bless you."

And then Jesus showed the ultimate kindness another way—by giving His life for us.

Kindness begins with God. He is kind to us, so we know how to be kind to others. When we're kind to people, they will want to show kindness to even more people—and it can spread throughout the whole world.

When we're kind, we show people what God is like.

When you let someone go before you in line, when you clean up a mess you didn't make, or when you help someone who's mean to you, you're showing how much God loves him or her.

When you talk to someone who's alone, give food to someone who's hungry, or pray for someone who's hurting, you're showing that person how good God is.

And there's one last thing you should know: you make God's heart happy when you do kind things. That's what He made you to do!

Little Faithfuls: You're So Kind

© 2020 Thomas Nelson

Tommy Nelson, PO Box 141000, Nashville, TN 37214

All rights reserved. No portion of this book may be reproduced, stored in a retrieval system, or transmitted in any form or by any means—electronic, mechanical, photocopy, recording, scanning, or other—except for brief quotations in critical reviews or articles, without the prior written permission of the publisher.

Published in Nashville, Tennessee, by Tommy Nelson. Tommy Nelson is an imprint of Thomas Nelson. Thomas Nelson is a registered trademark of HarperCollins Christian Publishing, Inc.

Tommy Nelson titles may be purchased in bulk for educational, business, fund-raising, or sales promotional use. For information, please e-mail SpecialMarkets@ThomasNelson.com.

ISBN 978-1-4002-1926-1 (eBook)

Library of Congress Cataloging-in-Publication Data is on file.

ISBN 978-1-4002-1924-7

Written by Carrie Marrs

Illustrated by Christiane Engel

Printed in China

20 21 22 23 24 DSC 10 9 8 7 6 5 4 3 2 1

Mfr: DSC / Shenzhen, China / July 2020 / PO #9585485

JOSEPH
- Went from being a slave to a leader in Egypt
- Could tell people the meaning of their dreams with God's help
- Took care of many people by saving enough food before a famine (a time when there is no food)

MIRIAM
- Was Moses' older sister
- Was a prophet (someone close to God who shared His messages with others)
- Was a musician who played instruments and sang praises to God

AARON
- Was Moses' older brother
- Was a good speaker and Moses' helper in freeing the Israelites from Egypt
- Was the first high priest in Israel

RUTH
- Was willing to leave her home country to stay with Naomi
- Worked hard in the fields so she and Naomi would have food
- Married Boaz, had a son, and became an ancestor of Jesus

JONATHAN
- Was the best friend David ever had
- Was a brave military leader
- Stayed loyal to God and to his friend David

ABIGAIL
- Was a problem-solver who saved lives before a battle started
- Made peace by changing David's mind when he was about to fight Nabal
- Married David after Nabal died